The Pocket Book of

POSITIVE AFFIRMATIONS

CONTENTS

Introduction

Positive affirmations are positive statements that you repeat to yourself. They are designed to help you change your negative thought patterns and beliefs into more positive ones. When you repeat positive affirmations, you are essentially telling yourself that you are capable, worthy, and deserving of good things.

Benefits of Practicing Positive Affirmations

- **Increased self-esteem:** Positive affirmations can help you to focus on your positive qualities and strengths, which can lead to increased self-esteem.
- **Improved confidence:** When you repeat positive affirmations to yourself, you are essentially telling yourself that you are capable and worthy of success. This can lead to improved confidence in your abilities.
- **Reduced stress and anxiety:** Positive affirmations can help to calm your mind and body, which can lead to a reduction in stress and anxiety levels.

- **Increased motivation:** Positive affirmations can help to give you the motivation you need to achieve your goals. When you believe in yourself and your abilities, you are more likely to take action and persevere in the face of challenges.
- **Improved mental health:** Positive affirmations can be helpful for people with a variety of mental health conditions, such as depression, anxiety, and low self-esteem. They can help to improve mood, reduce symptoms, and promote overall well-being.
- **Increased happiness:** Positive affirmations can help you to focus on the good things in your life and appreciate the present moment.
- **Improved sleep:** Positive affirmations can help you to relax and unwind before bed, which can lead to better sleep quality.
- **Enhanced creativity:** Positive affirmations can help you to feel more confident and open to new ideas, which can lead to increased creativity.
- **Improved relationships:** Positive affirmations can help you to be more positive and supportive in your relationships, which can lead to stronger and more fulfilling relationships.
- **Increased resilience:** Positive affirmations can help you to bounce back from setbacks and challenges, which can lead to greater resilience.

How to Practice Positive Affirmations

- **Choose affirmations that resonate with you.** The most effective affirmations are those that you truly believe in. Take some time to think about what you want to achieve and what you believe about yourself. Then, choose affirmations that reflect your values and goals.
- **Repeat your affirmations regularly.** The more you repeat your affirmations, the more likely you are to start believing them. Try to repeat them daily, or even several times a day.
  - **Write your affirmations down.** Writing your affirmations down can help you to focus on them and remember them more easily. You can put them on sticky notes around your house, in your journal, or on your phone.
  - **Find a mantra.** A mántra is a short, repetitive phrase that you can say to yourself to help you stay focused and positive. When you find yourself feeling negative or down, repeat your mantra to yourself.
  - **Meditate with your affirmations.** Meditation is a great way to quiet your mind and focus on your affirmations. You can either repeat your affirmations silently to yourself or out loud.

- **Say your affirmations with conviction.** When you repeat your affirmations, say them with conviction and belief. This will help you to internalize them and make them more powerful.
- **Visualize yourself achieving your goals.** When you repeat your affirmations, take some time to visualize yourself achieving your goals. This will help you to stay motivated and focused on your desired outcome.
- **Be patient and persistent.** It takes time to see results from using positive affirmations. Don't get discouraged if you don't see immediate changes. Just keep repeating your affirmations and eventually you will start to see a difference.

How to Identify that Your Positive Affirmations are Becoming a Reality

- **Pay attention to your thoughts and feelings.** When you are repeating your positive affirmations, pay attention to your thoughts and feelings. Do you feel more positive and optimistic? Do you feel more confident and capable?
- **Look for evidence in your life.** Are you seeing any positive changes in your life? Are you taking more action? Are you attracting positive people and experiences?
- **Talk to other people.** Talk to your friends, family, or therapist about your positive affirmations. See if they notice any changes in you.

Things you'll start to notice:

- **You start to believe in yourself more.** When you repeat positive affirmations, you are essentially telling yourself that you are capable and worthy of success. Over time, this can lead to a genuine belief in yourself and your abilities.

- **You start to take more action.** Positive affirmations can give you the motivation you need to take action and achieve your goals. You may find yourself setting goals and working towards them more often.
- **You start to notice positive changes in your life.** As you start to believe in yourself more and take action, you may start to notice positive changes in your life. You may find yourself feeling happier, more confident, and more successful.
- **You start to attract positive people and experiences into your life.** When you are positive and believe in yourself, you are more likely to attract positive people and experiences into your life. This can lead to new opportunities, relationships, and a more fulfilling life.
- **You start to feel more joy and gratitude.** As you start to see positive changes in your life, you may start to feel more joy and gratitude. You may appreciate the good things in your life more and be more content with your circumstances.

Confidence

Visualize yourself already being confident and successful.

- I am confident in my abilities.
- I am worthy of success.
- I believe in myself.
- I am capable of achieving anything I set my mind to.
- I am strong and capable.
- I am worthy of love and respect.
- I am enough just the way I am.
- I am a valuable and unique individual.
- I am worthy of happiness.
- I am a confident and powerful person.

Success

Visualize yourself already being successful.

- I am successful in everything I do.
- I am confident and capable.
- I am a hard worker and I never give up.
- I am open to new opportunities and challenges.
- I am surrounded by positive people who support my success.
- I am grateful for my successes, big and small.
- I am living my dream life.
- I am a beacon of light and inspiration to others.
- I am making a difference in the world.

Health

Visualize yourself already being healthy and vibrant.

- I am healthy and strong.
- My body is a temple and I treat it with respect.
- I eat healthy foods and I get enough exercise.
- I am grateful for my good health.
- I am healing from any illness or injury.
- I am surrounded by positive energy and healing vibes.
- I am open to receiving all the good that life has to offer, including good health.
- I am living a life of vitality and energy.
- I am happy and healthy.

Wealth

Visualize yourself already having the wealth you desire.

- I am worthy of financial abundance.
- I am open to receiving all the good that life has to offer, including money.
- I am grateful for the money I have, and I know that it will continue to grow.
- I am attracting more and more money into my life every day.
- I am a money magnet.
- I am good with money and I know how to use it wisely.
- I am generous with my money and I enjoy sharing it with others.
- I am financially free and I can do whatever I want with my money.
- I am living a life of abundance and prosperity.
- I am surrounded by wealth and I am grateful for all that I have.

Beauty

Visualize yourself already being beautiful, both inside and out.

- I am beautiful, inside and out.
- I am confident in my appearance.
- I love my body, flaws and all.
- I am grateful for my natural beauty.
- I am beautiful because I am unique.
- I am beautiful because I am kind and compassionate.
- I am beautiful because I am strong and independent.
- I am beautiful because I am intelligent and creative.
- I am beautiful because I am me.

Love

Visualize yourself already being in a loving relationship.

- I am open to love.
- I am worthy of love.
- I am a loving person.
- I attract loving people into my life.
- I am surrounded by love.
- I am grateful for the love in my life.
- I am confident in my ability to attract a loving partner.
- I am open to receiving love from others.
- I am a magnet for love.

Friendship ♥

Visualize yourself already having a strong and supportive network of friends.

- I am worthy of having good friends.
- I attract positive and supportive friends into my life.
- I am a good friend to others.
- I am open to making new friends.
- I am grateful for the friends I have in my life.
- My friends make me happy.
- My friends are there for me when I need them.
- My friends are supportive of my dreams.
- My friends challenge me to be a better person.

Family

Visualize yourself already being supported and loved by your family.

- My family is my biggest support system.
- I am grateful for my family.
- I am loved and supported by my family.
- My family is always there for me, no matter what.
- We are a team, and we can do anything together.
- I am proud to be a part of this family.
- I am learning and growing from my family.
- My family is a source of joy and laughter.
- I am blessed to have such a wonderful family.

Travel

Visualize yourself already having a positive and enjoyable travel experience.

- I am excited to travel and explore new places.
- I am confident in my ability to travel safely and independently.
- I am open to new experiences and cultures.
- I am grateful for the opportunity to travel and see the world.
- I am excited to meet new people and make new friends.
- I am looking forward to learning about different cultures and customs.
- I am confident that I will have a safe and enjoyable trip.
- I am grateful for the memories that I will make on my travels.
- I am a traveler, and I am proud of it!

Self-Esteem

Visualize yourself already being confident and self-assured.

- I am worthy of love and respect.
- I am enough just the way I am.
- I am a valuable and unique individual.
- I am capable of achieving anything I set my mind to.
- I am strong and capable.
- I am worthy of happiness.
- I am a confident and powerful person.
- I am grateful for my strengths and my weaknesses.
- I am learning and growing every day.
- I am loved and supported by others.

Self-Awareness

Visualize yourself already being self-aware.

- I am aware of my strengths and weaknesses.
- I am learning and growing every day.
- I am open to feedback and criticism.
- I am comfortable with who I am.
- I am accepting of my flaws.
- I am proud of my accomplishments.
- I am grateful for the challenges in my life.
- I am capable of achieving my goals.
- I am a valuable and unique individual.

Personal Growth

Visualize yourself already being the person you want to be.

- I am committed to my personal growth.
- I am open to new experiences and challenges.
- I am learning and growing every day.
- I am confident in my ability to achieve my goals.
- I am grateful for the opportunities for personal growth that come my way.
- I am patient with myself as I grow and change.
- I am forgiving of myself for my mistakes.
- I am proud of my accomplishments.
- I am excited for the future and all the personal growth that awaits me.

Inner Peace

Visualize yourself already being at peace.

- I am at peace with myself.
- I am calm and relaxed.
- I am in control of my thoughts and emotions.
- I am grateful for the good things in my life.
- I am surrounded by positive people and supportive resources.
- I am letting go of worry and anxiety.
- I am choosing peace over stress.
- I am living in the present moment.
- I am connected to my inner wisdom.

Inner Strength

Visualize yourself already being strong and capable.

- I am strong and capable.
- I am resilient in the face of challenges.
- I am not afraid to face my fears.
- I am confident in my abilities.
- I am a survivor.
- I am unstoppable.
- I am a force of nature.
- I am a warrior.
- I am a champion.
- I am strong enough to overcome any obstacle.
- I am strong enough to achieve my dreams.
- I am strong enough to handle whatever life throws my way.
- I am strong enough to be myself.
- I am strong enough to love and be loved.
- I am strong enough to make a difference in the world.

Resilience

Visualize yourself overcoming challenges.

- I am strong and capable of overcoming challenges.
- I am resilient and I bounce back from setbacks.
- I learn from my mistakes and I grow stronger.
- I am not afraid of change and I embrace new opportunities.
- I am supported by a strong network of people who believe in me.
- I have the power to choose my attitude and I choose to be positive.
- I am grateful for the challenges in my life because they make me stronger.
- I am capable of anything I set my mind to.
- I am a survivor.

23

Healing

Visualize yourself already being healed from trauma.

- I am strong and capable of healing from trauma.
- I am not alone. There are people who care about me and want to help me heal.
- I am worthy of love and happiness.
- I am learning and growing from my experience.
- I am letting go of the past and moving on with my life.
- I am creating a safe and supportive environment for myself.
- I am taking care of my physical and mental health.
- I am surrounded by positive people who lift me up.
- I am confident in my ability to overcome trauma.

Overcoming Emptiness

Visualize yourself already feeling full and fulfilled.

- I am not alone.
- I am worthy of love and happiness.
- I am capable of filling up my emptiness with positive experiences.
- I am learning and growing from my experience.
- I am letting go of the past and moving on with my life.
- I am creating a safe and supportive environment for myself.
- I am taking care of my physical and mental health.
- I am surrounded by positive people who lift me up.
- I am confident in my ability to overcome feeling empty.

Overcoming Regrets

Visualize yourself already living a life without regret.

- I am living my life to the fullest.
- I am taking risks and following my dreams.
- I am not afraid to make mistakes.
- I am learning and growing from my experiences.
- I am grateful for the opportunities that come my way.
- I am forgiving of myself for my past mistakes.
- I am letting go of my regrets and moving on.
- I am living in the present moment and enjoying each day.
- I am confident in my ability to create a happy and fulfilling life.

Overcoming Failure

Visualize yourself already achieving your goals.

- Failure is not the opposite of success. It is a necessary part of success.
- I am not a failure. I am simply someone who has not yet achieved their goals.
- I am learning from my failures and I am getting stronger every time.
- I am not giving up. I am simply changing my approach.
- I am confident that I will eventually achieve my goals.
- I am grateful for the opportunities that failure has given me to grow and learn.
- I am proud of myself for trying my best, even though I didn't succeed.
- I am not afraid to fail again. I know that I will eventually succeed.

Happiness

Visualize yourself already being happy.

- I am happy and content with my life.
- I am grateful for all the good things in my life.
- I am surrounded by love and support.
- I am living my life to the fullest.
- I am following my dreams and passions.
- I am making a difference in the world.
- I am healthy and vibrant.
- I am surrounded by positive people.
- I am open to new experiences.

Mental Health

Visualize yourself already having good mental health.

- I am worthy of love and happiness.
- I am mentally strong and resilient.
- I am strong and capable of overcoming challenges.
- I am capable of handling any challenge that comes my way.
- I am not afraid to face my fears.
- I am grateful for my mental health.
- I am taking care of myself physically and mentally.
- I am surrounded by supportive people.
- I am learning and growing every day.
- I am letting go of negative thoughts and emotions.
- I am creating a healthy and positive mindset.
- I am confident in my ability to achieve my goals.

Stress Management

Visualize yourself already being calm and relaxed.

- I am calm and relaxed.
- I am in control of my thoughts and emotions.
- I am able to handle any challenge that comes my way.
- I am surrounded by positive people and supportive resources.
- I am grateful for the good things in my life.
- I am taking care of myself physically and mentally.
- I am letting go of worry and anxiety.
- I am choosing peace over stress.
- I am living in the present moment.

Time Management 🕐

Visualize yourself already being a good time manager.

- I am in control of my time.
- I know how to prioritize my tasks.
- I am efficient and productive.
- I am focused and motivated.
- I am organized and prepared.
- I am able to say no to distractions.
- I take breaks when I need them.
- I am grateful for the time I have.
- I use my time wisely.

Anger Management

Visualize yourself already managing your anger effectively.

- I am in control of my anger.
- I am not my anger.
- I can choose how I react to situations.
- I am capable of calm and rational thinking.
- I am not afraid to express my feelings in a healthy way.
- I am surrounded by people who support me in managing my anger.
- I am learning and growing every day in my anger management journey.
- I am grateful for the opportunities to practice anger management.
- I am confident in my ability to manage my anger effectively.

Avoiding Procrastination

Visualize yourself already being productive.

- I am a productive person.
- I take action on my goals and dreams.
- I am not afraid of hard work.
- I am focused and determined.
- I am grateful for the opportunities to learn and grow.
- I am confident in my abilities to achieve my goals.
- I am not afraid to fail. I learn from my mistakes and keep moving forward.
- I am motivated to take action today.
- I am excited to see what I can accomplish.

Motivation

Visualize yourself already being motivated and focused.

- I am capable of achieving my goals.
- I am taking action towards my goals every day.
- I am learning and growing every day.
- I am surrounded by positive people who support me.
- I am grateful for the opportunities that come my way.
- I am excited about my future.
- I am confident in my abilities.
- I am unstoppable.
- I am a force of nature.

Career Growth

Visualize yourself already achieving your career goals.

- I am capable of achieving my career goals.
- I am learning and growing every day.
- I am taking on new challenges and responsibilities.
- I am networking with people who can help me advance my career.
- I am confident in my abilities and skills.
- I am open to feedback and criticism.
- I am persistent and determined.
- I am grateful for the opportunities that come my way.
- I am excited about my future career path.

Work-life Balance

Visualize yourself already having a healthy work-life balance.

- I am worthy of having a healthy work-life balance.
- I am capable of setting boundaries between my work and personal life.
- I am taking care of my physical and mental health, both at work and at home.
- I am spending quality time with my loved ones, both at work and at home.
- I am doing meaningful work that I am passionate about.
- I am surrounded by supportive colleagues and managers who understand the importance of work-life balance.
- I am confident in my ability to achieve my work goals while also maintaining a healthy personal life.
- I am grateful for the opportunity to have a fulfilling work-life balance.

Gratitude

Visualize yourself surrounded by gratitude.

- I am grateful for all the blessings in my life.
- I am grateful for my health, my family, and my friends.
- I am grateful for the opportunities I have been given.
- I am grateful for the challenges I have faced, as they have made me stronger.
- I am grateful for the lessons I have learned.
- I am grateful for the beauty in the world.
- I am grateful for the love and support I receive.
- I am grateful for the abundance in my life.
- I am grateful for the opportunity to make a difference in the world.

Made in the USA
Las Vegas, NV
22 April 2024

89015718R00024